World Cup Winners: Argentina

Striker Manuel Seoane

Playmaker Diego Maradona

WORLD CUP WINNERS

ARGENTINA

JASON OLSON

CREATIVE SPORTS

CREATIVE EDUCATION / CREATIVE PAPERBACKS

Published by Creative Education and Creative Paperbacks
P.O. Box 227, Mankato, Minnesota 56002
Creative Education and Creative Paperbacks are imprints of
The Creative Company
www.thecreativecompany.us

Book design by Blue Design (www.bluedes.com)

Images by Getty Images/Alessandro Sabattini, 5, Cui Nan/China News Service, 16, Dan Mullan, cover, 7, David Cannon, 15, El Grafico, 2, Elsa, 10, Julian Finney, 3, 20, Robbie Jay Barratt - AMA, 6, Simon M Bruty, 19; Pexels/Rafael Guimarães, 9; Wikimedia Commons/public domain, 1, 4, 12, 24

Library of Congress Cataloging-in-Publication Data
Names: Olson, Jason, 1981– author.
Title: Argentina / Jason Olson.
Description: Mankato, Minnesota : Creative Education and Creative Paperbacks, 2026. | Series: Creative sports. World Cup winners | Includes index. | Audience: Ages 7–10 | Audience: Grades 2–3 | Summary: "Led by soccer giants like Diego Maradona and Lionel Messi, Argentina won three FIFA World Cups. This elementary title follows "La Albiceleste" as they "tango" their way to soccer fame"– Provided by publisher.
Identifiers: LCCN 2024046120 (print) | LCCN 2024046121 (ebook) | ISBN 9798889895985 (library binding) | ISBN 9781682777640 (paperback) | ISBN 9798889896784 (ebook)
Subjects: LCSH: Soccer–Argentina–History–Juvenile literature. | World Cup (Soccer)–History–Juvenile literature.
Classification: LCC GV944.A7 O57 2026 (print) | LCC GV944.A7 (ebook) | DDC 796.334/0982–dc23/eng/20241212
LC record available at https://lccn.loc.gov/2024046120
LC ebook record available at https://lccn.loc.gov/2024046121

Printed in India

Defender Daniel Passarella

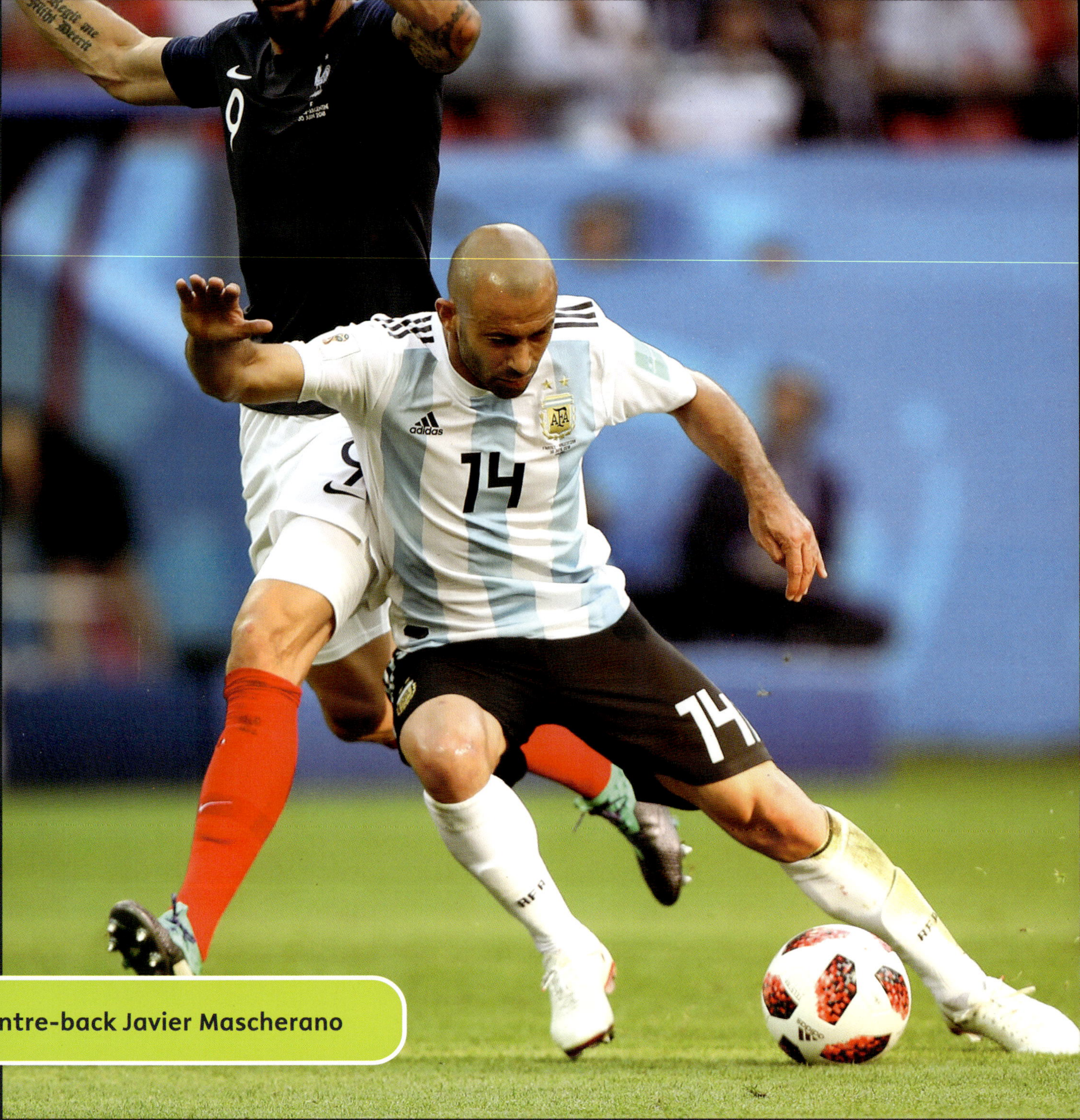

Centre-back Javier Mascherano

CONTENTS

Home of the Team

Argentina is the second-largest country in South America. Farmers raise cattle on its rich grasslands. Argentina is famous for a dance called tango.

Argentinians love soccer, and for good reason. Their national team is one of the few teams to have won the World Cup. The World Cup is a worldwide soccer tournament. Countries make teams of their best players. Every four years, they compete to become world champion.

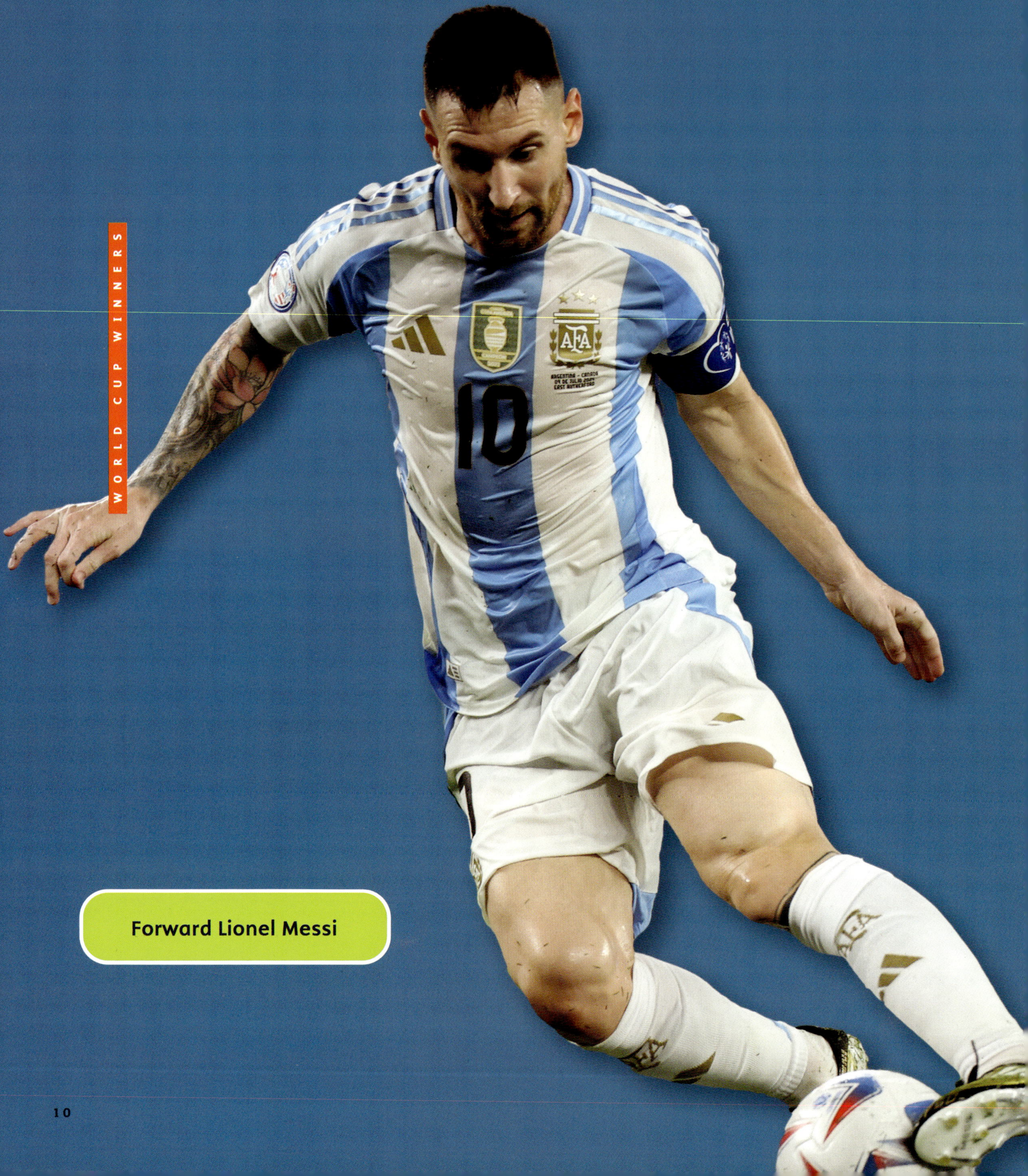

Forward Lionel Messi

Team Traditions

The Argentina national team is known as "La Albiceleste" ("The White and Sky Blue"). These are the colors of the team jersey. The team plays aggressive soccer.

Argentina's greatest **rival** is Brazil. When they play, it's called the "Battle of the Americas." Argentina's other rivals are England, Germany, and Uruguay.

Argentina vs. Uruguay, 1930

Team History

Argentina played Uruguay to a 6–0 win in their first match in 1902. The first World Cup took place in Uruguay in 1930. The South American neighbors and rivals played in the championship, with Uruguay winning 4–2.

In 1978, Argentina won its first World Cup, with players like Mario Kempes, Oswaldo Ardiles, and Daniel Passarella. Kempes scored twice in the final to beat the Netherlands 3–1. He scored six times in the tournament, winning the **Golden Ball**.

Argentina defeated West Germany 3–2 in the 1986 World Cup final to win its second trophy. The tournament was dominated by Argentina captain Diego Maradona. Among his most amazing goals, two came in a 2–1 win against England in the quarterfinals. They are known as the "Hand of God" and "Goal of the Century." Argentina went on the finish second in the 1990 and 2014 World Cups.

Playmaker Diego Maradona

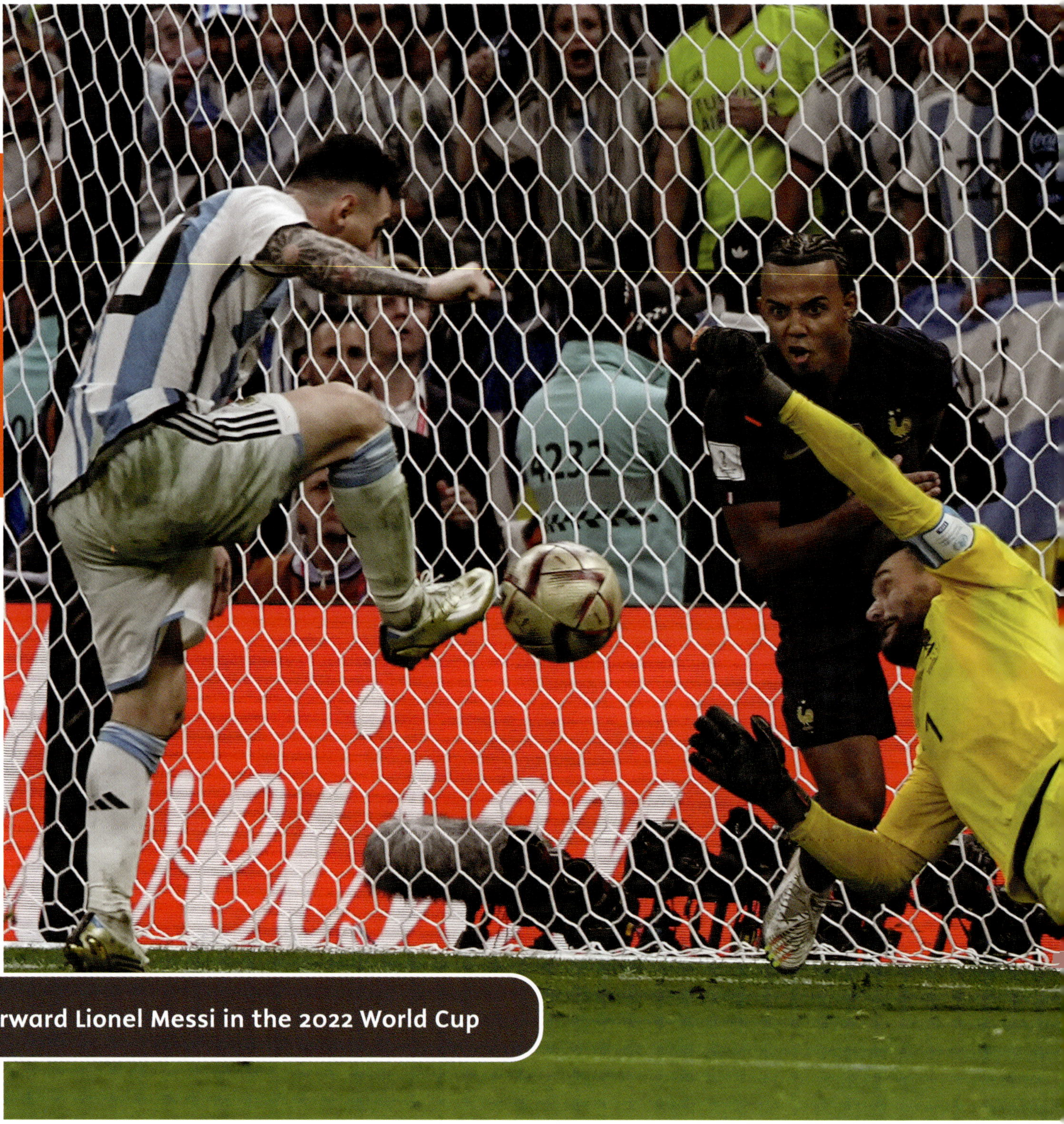

Forward Lionel Messi in the 2022 World Cup

Argentina won its third title in 2022. It faced France in the final. The match was tied 3–3 after extra time. Argentina won it 4–2 in penalties. Argentina captain Lionel Messi scored twice in the final—and seven times in the tournament.

WORLD CUP WINNERS

Team Stars

Each generation has a superhero. For some, that player is Maradona. For others, it's Messi. Both have become legends not only for their soccer skills but for winning the World Cup for Argentina.

Maradona played in four World Cups. He joined Brazilian legend Pelé as Player of the 20th Century. Messi played in five World Cups. He scored the most goals for Argentina (108 goals in 182 **caps**). Messi won two Golden Balls and eight **Ballon d'Ors**—far more than any other player.

Striker Gabriel Batistuta

ARGENTINA

Winger Ángel Di María

These superstars are not alone. Passarella won two World Cups with Argentina. Gabriel Batistuta scored 10 goals in three World Cups—second only to Messi's 13. Javier Mascherano and Ángel Di María played in four World Cups. Young players hope to match their example and win another trophy for Argentina.

About the Argentina National Team

First year: 1902

Team colors: white, sky blue

Home stadium: Estadio Mâs Monumental (El Monumental), others

WORLD CUP VICTORIES:

1978, 3–1 over the Netherlands

1986, 3–2 over West Germany

2022, 3–3, defeated France 4–2 in penalties

WEBSITE:

https://www.afa.com.ar/es/

Glossary

Ballon d'Or—an award given every year to the world's best soccer player

cap—an official match played for a national soccer team

Golden Ball—an award given to the best player in the World Cup

rival—a team that plays extra hard against another team

The first Argentina national soccer team, 1902

Index